FOUR GOOD
THINGS

The Houghton Mifflin New Poetry Series
Judith Leet, Pleasure Seeker's Guide
David St. John, Hush
Heather McHugh, Dangers
Gerald Stern, Lucky Life
Judith Wright, The Double Tree: Selected Poems 1942–1976
Christopher Bursk, Standing Watch
Thomas Lux, Sunday
James McMichael, Four Good Things

Also by James McMichael
Against the Falling Evil
The Lover's Familiar

FOUR GOOD THINGS

JAMES McMICHAEL

HOUGHTON MIFFLIN COMPANY
BOSTON 1980

Library of Congress Cataloging in Publication Data

McMichael, James, date
Four good things.

(Houghton-Mifflin new poetry series)
I. Title.
PS3563.A31894F68   811'.54   80–17157
ISBN 0–395–29913–6
ISBN 0–395–29914–4 (pbk.)

Printed in the United States of America

W 10 9 8 7 6 5 4 3 2 1

Portions of this poem have appeared in *Greenhouse Review,*
Paris Review, and *Ploughshares.*

I wish to thank the
John Simon Guggenheim Memorial Foundation
for their encouragement and financial help.

Linda Georgianna referred me
to the epigraph.

for Killarney, to whom it's told

Despise the world; despise nothing;
Despise yourself; despise despising yourself;
These are four good things.

— *the Abbess Herrad of Hohenburg*

FOUR GOOD
THINGS

From the McMichaels',
Florence. She passed the Silvers', the Johnsons'.
She was walking to Martello and the bus. She was
the woman who took care of me, and she was going
shopping.
   It was that one time in her life, a Saturday,
an afternoon. She was alone again. Glen was in
Tobruk, or somewhere, in the army, and it was years
after her first husband died, after the early
photograph in Eaton Canyon with the light
about where it was now. She had posed between
two oaks, the heel of each hand flat against them,
sleeves to her elbows, wind, the canyon to one side
dark at the falls where John Muir climbed and found
wild ferns and lilies, villages of wood-rats.
She'd gone only to the falls and come back out to
Pasadena, and the afternoon was just as late
now as it had been then. The sun was low and almost
blocked by the houses south of other houses
facing that way, as ours did. If she started
home again from downtown through the streets,
the houses that she passed between my room and there

1

were waiting for new tenants, for the doctor, for a
sober infirm neighbor of the Hales to stop
scorching his nose and forelock as he tried to
light his cigarette. If I heard her at the
back door with her packages, I knew that she would
soon start dinner. I'd watch, and she would let me
plead with her about the story of the fire,
give in and tell it, answer what I'd ask.
If I were with her, houses that my father sold
were possible, each at its certain distance from the
vineyard five blocks north. The mountain was absurdly
vertical and dark, and the cars that passed below it
droned in their stupor through the pepper trees.
Stick-piece-place, the stable with the horse and dog
were possible, remembered. Lights were going on in
other kitchens — yours before your parents moved there,
mine at some one time when Florence was with Glen.

How light it was outside was a matter
neither of us thought about. Florence went on
working at the sink. We talked and I kept
busy with the #20 New Connecticut grinder,
turned the crank and sent the bit along in
spirals, like a barber-pole. I took it apart,
followed its channel with my thumb and fit it
back in place securely with the wing-nut, tight.
I did all that again, each step, and we kept
talking. So that when we heard her car
and looked out past the palm tree to the street,

how light it was above the lawns or shrubs,
how far she'd driven or how far he had to drive
was easy, sure, and as composed as any
look she gave me when she came inside. She
talked with us a little, left us to our
interests in the kitchen. We heard his car
and knew that he was glad to be here, glad
for anything we had to tell him, and for her.
      He knew she'd live five years. She wouldn't
think about it, would be in and out of
wheelchairs, hospitals, assuming to the end
that she was getting better. That made it
tolerable for her, and covered him to work
so thoroughly at what he did all day
that coming home was easy. Dinner. Florence
leaving. Me in bed, asleep. Alone, it was
their time, unless the phone would ring. It would be
for him, some business matter, and would last
indefinitely while she did something else,
arranged the flowers for a still-life sketch,
wrote letters, read. I tell myself that
how they were with one another was as natural
as any hesitation, as their reluctance
ever to let me walk beyond the Johnsons'
or to school. If they were frightened or remote
they lived it over quietly, kept working,
made a long trip up the coast, with me.
I'd go to dinner with them at the Esterbrooks'.
To houses that he'd show on weekends with his sign
staked in the front lawn.

After she died, his business kept him longer.
Florence had moved away with Glen, and I was
there alone through the afternoons and early
evenings, into the hours when I'd listen
to the radio and wait to hear him drive in,
late. After ten, after my shows were over, I'd
worry every way he might be killed, would give it up
only and completely when his car was there.
With that exhilaration I could put on
all the calmness that I thought he wanted —
pretend to be asleep or answer tiredly
that I was there. I was certainly there, and
had been, hadn't been with him, wherever
he had been. But I didn't hate him for it,
loved him with a dull morose uncomplicated need
that made his days as strange to me as where he
spent them.
      That was the sense in which he was the city.
Two years before, he'd stepped off all its lots.
He'd mapped them, called them PASADENA TRACTS and
had them published, found they wouldn't sell.
Stacks of the copies sat there in his office.
He brought some home and I would look for
streets I knew, Paloma, Crary, Brigden Road.
He would be somewhere within his maps at any time —
at the office, mostly, on the phone about exchanges,
tax, big purchases of land for roads and public buildings.
Sales were what I understood. People moved
in and out of houses. Who they were,
what they cared about or did was less insistent

than the fact that they were there at any time for him.
They were his continuity as he was mine.
His listings of the houses up for sale had
pictures that were indistinct. I could make out
one or another, could place it from some
drive we'd taken. I'd see it as it mixed with
others that were occupied and were his business too.
They all made up a neighborhood, were part of that
difference from house to house that showed
more clearly in the mornings when the light
canted around the mountain, lifted, stayed
behind St. Lukes and lifted, took its time,
was fullest on the open porches, in some yards,
on streets like ours that paralleled the mountain,
east to west.

    He came home and got me and we drove
west, out Washington. Hill and Lake, Los Robles,
Lincoln, past a school. He told me they'd get
more than it was worth, and he would help them find
another house. Theirs would be torn down so the
school could be expanded. He understood their
wanting to stay. They had nine children.
I wanted it to take us longer to get there.
That way, they might be eating. He'd go to the door,
someone would let him in and they would talk.
I'd wait in the car and watch nothing, think
only about him coming out.
    But it wasn't late enough for that. We were

there already, and he made me come in too.
The rooms led off from this one toward the back,
upstairs, along a hallway to the right. Jimmie,
this was Mrs. Damiano. Earlier, on the phone,
he must have told her that I'd lost my mother,
that he felt he ought to take me with him,
sometimes, in the afternoon, like this.
She called her daughter, introduced us and
assigned her to me. The girl was older, poised,
knew what to ask me so she wouldn't seem
indifferent or burdened. I was in love with her.
I managed awkwardly a yes or no, felt overmatched
and homesick. I might have held on if I'd
kept myself from watching her. She would be
someone I could think about. Away from her,
in the car again and going home, I could
construe it some good way — no fantasy, no kiss,
but no ridiculous collapse like this one that was
coming on. She may have asked me what was wrong,
or even left me in a room upstairs while she
went down to say that I was crying, that I
wouldn't tell her what was wrong.

        I didn't know. It wasn't a conscious sadness.
I'd made him leave before he'd settled with them.
That didn't mean they'd get to stay. I didn't
care, or if I did I wanted there to be some
retribution. Nothing as clean as the wreckers
piling into it with their great ball. I think of this

now, and place some children there to watch —
not me, who was too old for that, nor any
younger Damiano whom I hadn't seen. Instead,
they'd be from several blocks away and would have
passed it in the weeks it sat there waiting.
They'd have the simple interest in its vacancy
that I have now, but would have wanted to
remember how the upper floor dropped through and
slammed and jostled as the sides were hit
again until it all came down and the trucks
collected it and took it off to burn.

      Two lovers walk out along a road in
Hampshire or Dorset, somewhere in the south.
On a small bridge, they stop without talking.
They are the narrative of their separate marriages
and have begun missing one another already.
Behind them, downstream, on the bank, a teacher
leads her file of students. She is telling them
"I want you to look closely at the river,"
and a few look dutifully and with good will
there, toward the middle, where she shows them that the
weed beds should be cut. She says the flow is
choking around the cups of water crowfoot,
that its surface should be undisturbed and
sometimes even sluggish, cramped, but not like this.
She points out plants along the margins,
the willowherbs and sedges, purple loosestrife, mint.
So they will stay away from it, she makes

each one of them touch once the spiny nettle-leaf.
They squeal and chatter and the lovers are
too far upstream to hear them and the place
between them, on the river, is again
more indivisible than either story. The people
leave within an hour. Even the teacher will forget
the deep unclouded pull below the catwalk
where a thin canal heads out and fills a
water-meadow of the flat. They leave,
and what each takes away is a distinct
autonomy to live and die, feel threatened or
ecstatic, tired, be someone I could come to
care about and yet be impotent to help or hurt
or to have love me with enough brute will to move
inside my need to be immune from things that
matter to me that I can't control.
        Rivers matter to me. I suppose my
carelessness in wading them is a romantic faith
that in a story they are only incidental.
Beyond the body of the suicide, the current
kept and changed its rhythm, hurried and turned
back and under and went on below whatever
rock had made that difference. Complying
evenly again with all the water, it was
nothing like the workers' hearts on seeing her,
nor like her own when she had just let go.
Like her heart now, the river was about itself
the way a vacant house can be about the
Damianos and go on as I would have it go,
not as a prop in an account with general

dispositions of the characters — that they moved
here or there within the city, didn't like the house
and moved away again as one by one the children
left and had their own lives somewhere else.
I'd have it go on as a house and use it as I
use a piece of music, investing it in no
deliberate or exacting way with my retreat from
people and their stories. I never asked my father
what became of them. I know the house was razed.
But I have kept it going on beyond its
natural and even just conclusion, kept it as
possessively as if its being vacant made them mine,
denied their separateness and let me find them
anywhere, in any other house that was as big.
I wasn't looking for them. On the distracted
walks I'd take as a naive voyeur, I had
forgotten them and what the house itself was like.
My finding them unrecognized was that much more
secure and comforting. Because I had to deal with
nothing but a house or houses, I could be
closed off from what they held and have that mean
precisely that they couldn't hurt me. If I
think of all the houses, I don't know which ones
had made me want to take those walks. The old
three-story place on Hill and Mountain was too
obviously dark and gothic, almost funny,
its finials and stained glass like a fairy tale,
a house that some rich lawyer with a lot of kids
might buy and renovate. Others that were set
much deeper on their lots, behind the trees, were more

anonymous. They gave me nothing to oppose —
no walks nor entryways, no lights that I could see
at some one angle as I tried to know if
anyone was there. They were or weren't, and either way
it didn't matter since I couldn't see to will them
back into the back rooms where they would say and do
the things that were their story. I wanted that
suggestiveness that even smaller houses had —
a living room illumined, empty, someone coming
inside from the patio to get the phone.

     My mother was dying. I didn't know that,
didn't know why I couldn't be at home when she had
left the hospital to be there. He would
take me to Lucile's and leave me and I'd hate it.
I'd worry that I'd have to stay and go on
living there like one of hers, like Donna, Elva,
Polly, and Dwight. I thought my father knew I
blamed them somehow when my mother died. And, too,
Lucile was his cousin. So when she moved from
Oak Knoll to a bigger place on Holliston,
and when we'd go to see them on the weekends
and would eat there, work together on the house,
when he'd been sick one time just after Christmas
and had slept with her downstairs while I had
stayed awake outside Dwight's room, in the hall,
when Florence even told me what was coming,
told me, as she said, "explicitly" what they would do,
I no more thought about his marrying Lucile

than I had thought my mother wouldn't live.
We moved from Cooley, they were married. Like Dwight,
I had three older sisters and was lonely, vain.
There wasn't any closeness. They had the same
detachment and reserve with one another
that they had with me. The five of us were all
polite enough and did the housework with our
moderate displays of bitching. We saw to it
always that each other's messages got through.
We never interfered, fought only in the
petty ways of adolescents. Donna was loud,
Elva and Polly quiet. If any of the four of them
resented me they didn't show it, seemed
genuinely to like my father, as they always had.
I hated them. I hated Lucile. After that
death, that first one, possibly the last death
ever to surprise me, I'd been surprised again.
I knew I'd left things out when I had worried,
and I hated them for being part of that.
My father seemed as lost to me as if he'd died.
It didn't matter what I felt. We had become
conspicuously a family with any family's
collective will. I'd go on living with them
in a house that they had lived in first.

The mountain north of Pasadena has severe
and angular back canyons where the light is always
unexpected, out of place, too simple for the
clutter of the granite blocks along the creeks.

The slopes have low rough shrubs, some firebreaks.
It rains sometimes, and then the soils wash easily
through Rubio and Eaton canyons to the small
catch-basins and the storage tanks. The bedrocks
tilt toward the west, and so the seepage
drains that way. Along a wall of the Arroyo,
it comes down in springs named Tibbets, Ivy,
Flutterwheel. These are the only steady water,
and the Indiana colony had hauled it out
in tubs and barrels to their lots. They'd cleared
the greasewood from the flats and planted groves of
orange and peach trees, built their houses in the
California Style with battened redwood boards.
Nearer the Arroyo, on its terraces,
they saved a few live oak. They'd have December
picnics there and afterward would walk from
that side, down the bluff. The floor was cool,
and there were sycamore and alder, loose
irregular new channels through the willows.
On the other side, and south, below the San Rafaels,
more oak, the sun. They'd take a new way back.
      Their lots extended east to the Lake Vineyard
Land and Water Company. And as a grudging
compromise between that tract and theirs,
the Central School was built in the dry neat
rows of the orchards east of where they lived.
Excursion parties from the Middle West were taken
mostly with the climate. At the citrus fairs,
the charts and produce showed them that it didn't freeze.
Storms were rare and offered the consoling interest

of a flood in the Arroyo, loud and stupid
boulders the size of safes colliding down the wash.
A new hotel faced south on Colorado. Like the
Ward Block to its right across Fair Oaks,
it was substantial, frame, with dormers and
brick chimneys. Each had its widow's walk
and looked as much like Boston as it needed to.
Someone from Los Angeles brought in a telephone.
He hooked it up in the store on the southeast corner,
rode back downtown and called and asked for
so-and-so, who wasn't there. From that one
crossing, there were fewer lots each month,
new storefronts and more traffic, speculating
boomers and pikers, midnight sales, bands and free
lunches at the auctions. Owners were induced to move
east on Colorado to more eligible locations,
but the cross-streets led through dusty tent-lined
orchards to the chaparral. The boom came back
toward the center and was done. What they'd been
selling was the weather and a place to live, and
that was what was left. As their one industry,
the Novelty Works of Mr. Wakeley went on stuffing
scorpions and trapdoor spiders, horny toads,
small animals and birds. The balance of trade was
not in Pasadena's favor.
      But there were jobs. James Scoville kept men doing
rockwork on the banks above his groves. The Arroyo
narrowed there, and so he had them build a
pumphouse and a dam and turn a railroad trestle
upside down between two concrete footings.

This was the central bridge. It crossed to open
ranchland that would subdivide more slowly than the
woodlots on the bluffs. Another bridge, La Loma,
farther south, was taller, with a wider span and
sycamores around its girders. It had replaced the
Johnston bridge and made it easier to sell the tracts.
The wealth of the invisible elite went into homes on
Grand and Orange Grove, Raymond, Nithsdale Rd.,
Arroyo Terrace, Bellefontaine, new bungalows
that looked much less expensive than they were.
In their commissions, Charles and Henry Greene
used common and available materials,
stones from the Arroyo, bricks, a simple flexible
pine frame of 2 x 4s and hand-split cedar shakes,
porches that were railed with the same rough timber
as the posts and beams and trusses and the overhanging
rafters for the roof. Their costs were mostly labor.
They'd show the workers where they wanted
terraces and knolls, what trees and shrubs to save.
A local factory expanded to keep up with them,
and they'd make daily visits there to oversee
the millmen and the carvers or the quality of
lumber that had just been shipped. Their mason did
exactly what they called for on retaining-walls,
the color of the fill, which stone or clinker at what
angle to the rest. Each minor thing they cared about
earned what it had to do with matters that were
not their business. Where the money for a house had
come from, what the Mayor had in mind, or
Public Works, or how the street would look with lights —

affairs like these beyond the garden stayed
accessible, a movement to and from the house
implicit in its horizontal lines. The roof was
long and relatively flat. Beams above the frames of
doors and windows were much broader than the
frames themselves and paralleled the covered
entryways and porches. Even the stairs inside
were less than vertical, each section of the railing
carved from a single piece of teak and joined to
all the other teak — the notched and interlocking
kickplates, the splines and level boards that were
the facing of the well. Their stairs were furniture.
A bench along a landing had the same insistent
finish as the inglenook, the same square
ebony caps for screwheads as the chairs and tables.
Everything showed you how it went together.
A scarf or box-joint, metal straps, continuous
sure banding from the hallway into any room.
There was tile and leaded glass, but it was mostly
wood — mahoganies and walnuts, oak, redwood or
white cedar wainscots, doweled and pegged loose
furniture in teak or birch or lignum-vitae, a smooth
self-lubricating wood that didn't crack. The grain
inside was outside too in rafters and stiff rounded
beam-ends that were oiled and rubbed. They looked
penetrable to light, looked as if they could
absorb and carry it at any single time toward the
one best place inside. Lucile's house on Holliston
was miles from the Arroyo. But it was imitation
Greene & Greene, a less impressive version of their

simplest large two-story frames. Its eaves on
both the north and south reached almost to the
neighbors' lots, lots that for several blocks each way
repeated themselves with slightly different houses.
The man she'd bought it from was still a
pharmacist at Lake and Villa. He didn't know me
and I never spoke to him. He had a massive
tumor on his neck and jaw, and I would be
amazed each time I saw him that he wasn't dead.
Until a year or so before he'd sold the house,
there'd been an organ with the pipes extending to an
upstairs bedroom, probably the room across the hall from
Donna's. There would have been no floor between
the first and second stories, our den and sewing room
a single shaftlike chamber that the sound would fill.
It's just as likely that the floor had been there
all along, exactly as we knew it, with the organ
somewhere else. But of all the rooms downstairs,
only the den could open to the room above it.
With the ranks of pipes along the wall that
backed against the stairs, there would have been
high windows to the south and west, and possibly,
around three sides, a thin railed walk one got to
from the upstairs hall. I might let myself care
more about how well or what he played if it were
clearer to me how the organ looked. If I know
anything about its wood, I know it from the
oak-frame sliding doors between the den and
living room. So if the console had been quartered oak,
the case was walnut — no tracery around the pipes,

the same plain cuts as for the cabinets and counters
everywhere downstairs. How many manuals there were,
or knobs with nameplates for the pitches and the stops,
if the bench was free or fixed, or whether the
pedals for the naturals were strips that flared
slightly in their alignment toward the darker sharps —
the whole clear shape of it in that one place remains as
closed to me as how it worked, as the feeders and the
reservoirs, the valves, the layers of coarse felt between
the double panels of the swell-box; as how the sliders
kept the air below the upper-boards and pipes
and let it go and let it sound the way he
wanted it to sound, the wind inside the pipe
striking against a lip and coming back, contained and
vibrant for the time he kept it there. Its shock to the
air outside the pipe was how it sounded, the way he
wanted it to sound, or as it might have sounded
if the room were larger and the sounds dispersed and mixed
less palpably, went on together with the light or
darkness in the room. There wouldn't have been time
between the sounds to count them to be sure that
nothing of the piece was missing. Nor was there time
for me, at any moment in the sewing room, to know
the changes that the light had worked downstairs.
Not that I would have tried to know, or done much more
than suffer my current fit of pouting. I'd hear Lucile
walk past the stairs toward the kitchen in her busy
self-important way. Maybe she'd leave. From a back
window of the sewing room, I'd see her in her car and
starting out the driveway. These were the least

obstructed windows in the house. Late in the day,
haze showed its tired agreement with the house next door,
the shingles dull and olive like the rusted screens, the
asphalt paper on the roof. I could see my aunt's
back yard on Chester. Trees as far west of us as Lake
marked off the streets in staggered elevations — palms,
short rows of deodars and jacarandas. At night,
from a window in the southern wall, the top three
letters on the tower for the ACADEMY kept coming on
one at a time, then all together.

    Before I moved there, while Dwight still had a
bedroom to himself, the upstairs hall had opened to
a sleeping porch. We closed the hall with a partition,
made a second smaller room that gave us closets and a
place for desks. It was the only access to the porch,
and I could leave that way by getting to the roof and
dropping from its lowest corner to the lawn.
But the roof had better uses. From its apex, I could
lift myself another level to the eave above the porch
where there were windows to the attic. I'd take one off
and crawl inside along the boards toward the open
hatch in the bathroom ceiling. No one would hear me.
Or back outside the attic, from the eave,
I'd use the beam-end as a hoist and pull myself
over the rafter to the highest roof. It had
good footing, a broad low pitch and several vents.
I don't know why I'd go there — maybe for the sublime
assurance that I could. Being there was almost to be

doing something. The sky went on at that one level,
intervened below the trees and rooflines and withdrew.
There was more to see than I could choose from,
the tallest buildings, like the Star-News and the City Hall,
too obvious to use as landmarks. I could climb back
down again with no clear sense of what I'd seen and go
collecting for the paper. People were home, and I'd be
nervous and abrupt, or sometimes pass the house for
others where there might not be an answer. I'd
fantasize about a friend of Polly's or the girl
somebody's brother fucked two times before her father
caught them at it and apologized and went away.
Sex was as foreign to me as a sense of how to
talk to people. I'd been born into a neighborhood of
older couples, widows, three or four small families
with teen-age sons or daughters whom I'd tried to know.
Florence thought they were too old for me.
My dealings with them were as strange as that one time
behind the Coles' with Jan and Helen when he told me
privately to touch her here. I hadn't understood
and botched it, made her angry at me, knew a little
better what he'd meant when he was giving her a
long and proper feel-up, which she seemed to like.
By now, I was as old as Jan had been. He'd seemed to
know what he was doing. I knew I didn't know,
and was convinced that my not knowing left me out.
The vagueness of the city when I looked at it
was my exclusion from the lives that made it clear.
People wanted it to look the way it did. The common
steady houses were their parts — lumber and stucco,

glass, the indeterminate and easy changes.
Streets were so well cared for and had so much shade
that they seemed more than what they were, or less,
another vaguer thing, the leisure, maybe, to be
somewhere else, a promise or perhaps a claim that
differences are good or never matter. I let it
keep what might have been its quality without me,
that "frightening calm" that Pasadena has for you,
its people there or not, inside their houses and in
no one place.

     What did people do all day? I never asked that,
but I'd go downtown where there were people whom I
didn't have to talk to or to know. They were
shoppers and clerks and never seemed to catch me
watching myself in the parade of storefront windows.
I wasn't there for any reason. Every week or so
I'd go to a shop upstairs on Green and steal more
stamps from the show-books while I chose a few to buy.
She'd bring them to the counter — all the British
Colonies in the Americas: Antigua, Virgin Islands,
St. Kitts-Nevis, Montserrat. From the Bahamas,
a new series of eleven, clean, bicolored, all
consistently engraved. The ½d orange and slate-grey
Infant Welfare Clinic. Modern Dairying. And
Native Straw Work. Water Sports. A Fishing Fleet.
Out Island Settlement, with a bay and dock and
warehouses at odd angles, some of their roofs
the color of the paper, like the sky, the others

close consecutive dark lines. Each stamp had the same
embossed and perfect border. The Queen looked
pleased, but not at what the stamp was showing us
and not at us.

   Scott's Catalogue and Album were at home,
and I still have them both, the stamps in their places in
flat tubes of cellophane, each checked against its
mint or canceled value in the catalogue. I've
counted them, 612, a third from Canada, the rest
from twenty-two crown colonies in the Atlantic or the
Caribbean. These islands were anachronistic
baggage of the slave and sugar trade, geographies of
simple dockets, bills of lading, ports, and putting in.
The manufacturers had wanted more. They drank to
"Markets! Markets!" at their dinners, and for
Christmas 1898, Joe Chamberlain had given them
a penny postage and a stamp that said "WE HOLD A
VASTER EMPIRE THAN HAS BEEN." They hadn't learned
that properties and goods were not enough,
that the sum of what they held was still a sum of
limits — land and factories and ships and
things that needed places: calicoes, bright shirts,
Stoke potteries and Sheffield knives. Even their
revenues were less than time, less than the
pure investment that the Germans made in knowing
everything — the languages of all their clients,
tastes, the smallest and most incidental changes in
production and the tariffs. Unlike Great Britain,
Germany and the United States were planners. Each
consolidated all its worries, tried to organize

the clutter of the unpredictable to make it
go their way. What went wrong in either war was
personality — bad planning what went wrong between.
Von Kármán's tunnel at Cal Tech could simulate the
turbulence a wing would meet in flight. It told him
which designs had possibilities and futures.
Growth was the provision of the time it took to
know that what was planned was right because it
earned more time to plan. Because the "Gibson Girl"
was heavy, bulky, had a kite-antenna and a crank,
an Army-Navy "E" Production Pennant went to
Hoffman Radio who planned and made a two-way
voice and code transceiver, which was small.
Their corporation flourished when the war was over.
They kept some military contracts, hired more engineers
who narrowed every unit of their work on TV
kinescopes and circuits. The beams of cathode-ray
electrons through a vacuum tube would synchronize each
thirtieth of a second. Successively, in league,
they looked like something. So that if you'd
wanted to, you might have seen what looked like
water, a level vaguely like the air between
the hybrids of white lilies. Seen bamboo, the
culvert where the pond filled. A slope with
ferns in the wet hollows, shade, the pouched winged
irises in their black pools under the trees.
Rough grass between some steps, the seedlings rooting
deep into the bank along the cool backs of the stones.
There was sun here, and poplars beyond the high
clipped hedges and the wall. You couldn't see the

teahouse or the smooth flagged path that had been
washed down carefully, fine residues of soil
still drying at the borders. There wasn't any wind.
From the street, the door of a garage pulled
up and back and a light went on inside,
reflected from the clean paint of the driveway.
A man in a white tuxedo left his house.
Someone smelled gardenias as she found her mailbox
locked with a lock she hadn't put there, its numbers
filed away illegibly, impossible to trace.
The son of a man I worked for died of a
bubble in his blood-stream. As a messenger,
one week near Sixth and Main, he'd seen a man
on fire and heard a window-washer scream and fall
ten stories to the sidewalk. When he went home,
his aunt was dead in the bathtub. He made the
phone-call, ate some cheese, began to walk around
unlike himself and asking quietly "Is everyone
all right? Is everyone all right?"

    With my conception, I was virtually
coincident with cancer in my mother's body.
To exist is to be *placed outside*, where there are
things to fear. My body. Me. The visible
pulse at my right ankle, thick blue vein, the skin,
sunlight on my ankle in a cold house, now.
When I'm afraid, I try to think of everything.
I try to change the possible by thinking some one
part of it and giving it a place — gratuitous

murder, accident, a flood, the separate and bizarre
pathologies that could be mine and final.
Worry is somewhat less possessive, less complete,
more frequent and deliberate, self-amused. It too
displaces where I am with something that I make
inside me. Each thing I worry is secure,
familiar, almost home. Its difference is
mine and not the world's. The house wren, when it sings, says
"Here I am." It looks around and says it.
My worrying and fear are notices that I don't
have a place outside and don't know how to
find or make one. They are as free of people as a
garden is, or as a plan.
        When my father died five years ago, Lucile
sold the house on Holliston and went to live with
Polly for a while. I was glad she was moving.
Pasadena would be less a place I'd go to
see someone I knew, be more the way I
wanted it to be — continuous, immune, with
incidental people. I'd spend the hour it takes
to drive there, park the car and walk up
Holliston and past the Nehers'. Theirs was
one of the houses that would plant itself
inside me when I'd read *The Life of Constable*, and
Roughing It, and *Madame Bovary*. Into the books that
pointed with interest to a certain place,
one of those places that I felt I knew would
intervene — not clearly, nor for any longer than
my time in walking past it. I wouldn't try to
keep it out or learn what it was doing there. I'd

commandeered it as a simple place, and what went
on inside it was as safe and constant as the
book itself. And since it wasn't just the Nehers',
since there were other houses too, what I was
after wasn't any single house but was instead the
possibility of houses, the abstruse sum of all
possible houses in that city, all of them
mine and filled with incidental people whom I
covered with my version of the Yahweh: I WHO AM
AM, and so the rest of you can be.

  I know that it's otherwise — myself and other
unimagined people, their lives and mine, yours.
You had your own life there without my having
worried or imagined it, your difference
outside me, like the places that I know but more
surprising, more like those places that are
much more yours than mine. Like the Arroyo,
Mayfield, or Pacific Oaks. Like Bellevue Dr.
and Euclid, and St. Andrews — as far toward the
north and east in Pasadena as there were
houses that I didn't know. There'd be the streets that
neither of us thought about. Those that we had
were quiet and homogenous with now and then a
grocery store, a park, each street familiar but
indefinite within the strict geography of the
Arroyo, and the mountain, and those clear
aristocratic boundaries to the east and south.
In our stuntedness with people, what they
wanted for themselves resisted any little that we
made of it. What people did all day was

work of different kinds. On Altadena Dr.,
near Cooley, Roma Mulvihill consulted with her
botanist about the tree-ferns and the epiphytes,
a cool thick air inside her greenhouse as the
girls were dusting bronzes in the shop.
Scripps College was presented with the Charles Yale
Memorial Collection of fine presses, first editions,
and his specialties: The West, and Californiana.
At Aerojet, Fritz Zwicky thought about his
template of the stars for Project Rosy Glow.
Friends of my father's went on Tuesday Morning
Breakfast Tours of houses up for sale. Another friend,
"Rex" Rucklos, kept on looking for the men who needed
money and knew how to use it. H. Leslie Hoffman's
Easy-Vision Lens gave sharper contrasts. While he
arranged a point of sale or worked a coup for
college football, wrestling, and a recent film,
his tubes were mounted in blond cabinets and shipped.
Lyman Stewart's grandson was Executive Vice
President of Union Oil. J. T. McGucken had been
Papal Chamberlain, Domestic Prelate, and was now
Most Reverend Bishop, Vicar General of the Diocese.
Russ Peak, who made a fly-rod for the President.
The owners and employees of The Glass House,
Lytle's Roofing, Brotherton's, Crown City
Mattresses and Infants Socks. Clerks under the
diamond skylights at J. Herbert Hall's. Deliverymen
with the harried confidence to park their trucks in
anybody's driveway. People were home and working.
Harlo Mills, my piano teacher. Florence. Mrs. Shade.

You were home, your sense of what you knew extending
less as a line of places than as mornings
oddly alike and anywhere. And you were busy.
You were another person doing chores and things we
all do privately as what might happen to us
happens or doesn't.

      Richard Arkwright was a barber. He toured the
markets and the farms and bought the hair of
country girls and made it into wigs. When he
hired John Kay to build a frame for spinning
thread from the strands of cotton, manufacture was
domestic — looms and jennies in the kitchens of the
small freeholders and the farmers who would
sell their cloth to merchants. Wool was the English
staple trade, a privilege of the landed graziers.
All gentlemen wore silk. Raw cotton was a coarse
adherent fiber from Brazil and the Antilles.
It had to be opened and cleaned and have its strands
laid parallel by two large cards that worked it
back and forth between them. Drawing made the slivers
equal in thickness by redoubling them, and roving
made them thicker still and left them ready to be spun.
Arkwright's water-frame replaced the hand's inexpert
pulling and pushing, movements that begin and end
and can't repeat themselves exactly. At Cromford,
with the money of two hosiers, he built a gas-lit
mill above the Derwent. He needed journeymen
clockmakers who did tooth and pinion, a smith who

forged and filed. Afraid that no one man would know
"all that I should expect he might," he was
"determined to let no person see the works." He wanted
"locks and hangings for the windows; good latches
for the outer doors, and for the inner doors as well."
To make the other money come to him,
he specified as little as he could in all his
patents. And as he sold the plans, he built six
factories in Lancashire. At Glasgow, he was made
an honorary burgess and was taken to the
Falls of Clyde, at New Lanark, where he would
build another mill. He advertised for weavers,
framework-knitters. Children who were seven could have
constant employment. In the riots against machines,
they burned his mill near Chorley. He was threatened:
"I will lie in wait for you in this town Nottingham
or wherever I most likely to find you. I will
ashure shute you as your name is what it is.
Dam you do you think the town must be ruled by such a
barber as you." Contemporaries thought he was
a Newton or Napoleon. He was knighted and named
High Sheriff of Derbyshire. He claimed that
he could pay the national debt if he were
left alone to make his money; and when he died,
the income from his mills was more than that of most
German principalities. He was asthmatic. An
economist of time, he worked at English grammar as he
traveled in a post-chaise with four horses driven
always at top speed.

   He lost his patents at a trial in 1785.

The industry was open. In the damp valleys,
at breaks in the long profiles of the streams,
new spinning mills went up. They were too far
outside the towns to worry that they'd be
inspected — close enough to send their thread
to upland workshops by the new trans-Pennine
turnpike roads, or by the new canal that crossed the
valley of the Calder, through the Craven drumlins
east to the other watershed, and Leeds.
There was so much thread that barns were fitted up with
handlooms that could weave good fustians and cambrics.
Cotton was its own new country, and the landlords
feared the moneyed men. Land could itself be
capital, the business of the aristocracy.
Each landlord had his broken straggling plots,
their furrows running lengthwise to the rounded
headlands where the plough would turn. He knew
which land was his, but it was open and was grazed
collectively by several owners. Between
harvest and sowing, even his farmers' pigs would
graze there with the sheep. Cows grazed the catchwork
meadows on the terraces, or at the watersides.
Enclosure was the landlords' plan to change their
strips of arable to larger straighter fields.
They would appropriate the wastes — the marshes and moors,
the peat-bogs where the farmers got their fuel.
Commons had been "a profit which a man hath in the
land of another, as to pasture beasts thereon,
cut wood, catch fish, hunt coneys, and the like."
In most of the Midland parishes, there were now

Acts for Enclosure of the Open and Common Fields,
new roads with wide grass verges to a ditch,
then quickset hedgerows, ash, occasional small
farmsteads with a croft, no lanes, the landlord's
manor and his park, and in the fields the
thickets for his foxes. It cost him less to
graze than till. The stiff clay soils would hold
a year of wheat, another of spring corn, lie fallow.
The land would yield him more if he could save
the labor of his farmers and the cottagers.
Tenure at Will was his prerogative to put them
off the land when he was through with them.
As he engrossed more farms, they set his hedges,
drained and marled the looser tracts and planted
clover, turnips, and lucerne. He managed
breeds of stock and turned them out to graze the even
turf across the hillocks. Enclosure had made
"fat beasts, and lean poor people." With no one skill
peculiar to themselves, they left the villages for
workshops in the north. The Earl of Leicester said
"I look around and see no other house than mine.
I am like the ogre in the tale, and have eaten up
all my neighbors."

        Although you couldn't have because of other luck,
if you'd come in from Stockport through the fields
south of the Medlock, you'd have passed the first few
villas and their lamp-lit oval drives, your father
looking for a brickcroft and a kiln where you could sleep.
How much we'd know about you now would turn upon
how far you'd come. Your name could mean that you'd

crossed over in a packet-boat from Cork for the
summer harvests, hay, then peas, then onion-pulling,
working north with other navvies as the crops
ripened or were taken by the frost. Near the Potteries,
more tramways with their loads of coke, more furnaces,
white tips and slag-heaps at the edges of the fields.
There were fewer of you, and then just your family.
You'd found a recess in a viaduct, some driftwood,
scraps, but no soup-kitchen. Tomorrow night, you'd
be here on the outskirts in the kiln and thinking
God knows what about the possibilities for
any of you, warmth, or health, whatever other
standard things we might suppose that you'd have liked,
a peep-show caravan, or suet puddings.
Little Ireland was across the Medlock on the Oxford Road,
and you were all up early. For as long as you had
jobs to find, the streets would keep you looking
further into what was there beyond the frontages.
Through the entrance to a foundry, you could see the
dockside — cranes, a horse-dray, narrow boats,
the water out of your view below the worn stone
curbing of the wharves. The back-to-backs, doors
open to the floor inside: a chimney and staircase,
the bed a heap of straw with quilts of old sacking.
A woman told your father he and Wick could try
"that warehouse. The mills in Ancoats for the
lady and the girls." If you'd been taken on there,
we'd have lost you to the city as you'd found it,
Jersey Street, The Phoenix Works, long rows of looms with
straps from a central shaft, the oil, steam, the

operatives and overlookers, a flour-and-water
paste between your fingers as you dressed the warp.
We'd have lost how you were different from what you'd
done to stay alive. And as you'd stayed alive,
you would have been the things you'd known, things that we can't
recover, that we tend instead to think of
as examples of a tyranny, bad luck. We know that
courtyards from the narrow alleys were as
hard to find as they were rotten and undrained,
dark, with offal-heaps, small pens for pigs, a doorless
privy where the modest brought their feces in a shoe.
We know that there were eight or ten to every
room off these courts. Doors were their ventilation and
stayed open to the passages where everything lay
quietly where it was thrown. People were living in the seams —
in undercrofts of bridges and along the
rivers and canals where they would bathe, the water
warm from the boiler-tailings, dyes, and bleaches,
from the refuse that would lift through floors
of houserows slipping toward the Irwell and the Irk.
Crosses on the Ordnance Maps of 1850 mark the streets
where five or more had died of typhus. Workers ate
only the tainted meats. Their foodstuffs were
adulterated: flour, with chalk or gypsum; pounded
nutshells in the pepper, sloe-leaves in the tea.
Mothers were back at work the same day they delivered,
milk dripping from their shirts. Each wet nurse
had a dozen babies. She'd give them Quietness —
a dose of treacle, sugar, and crude opium —
and they would look much older than they were.

They'd go to work as menders in the mills. After their shifts,
too tired or too accustomed to the heat,
they'd sometimes hide away in drying-rooms and
sleep there and be roused and, still asleep,
start going through the movements of their trade.
Andrew Ure had seen them at the looms. He'd found it
"delightful to observe the nimbleness with which they
pieced the broken ends in that few seconds'
exercise of their tiny fingers." Habit had given them
" a pleasing dexterity." They were "lively elves
whose work resembled sport." It didn't look that way to
Engels. Children were in the mills because the jobs took
"cursory attention." Skills made a worker more
intractable and less dependent. As long as there were
"workers enough, and not all so insane as to prefer
dying to living," their master had it as he wanted it.
He had the capital to shield himself against
uncertainties within the market. And when those came,
the workers were displaced and worked for less and were
"as much without volition as the rivers."
Nor was the family a place for them. Children took their
parents' jobs. A family would last as long as
any of its members needed it for his or her own
interests. One family was all those people who might
unionize and ask their master what he meant to
do with them. His was another family. It was as
different from theirs as any printer of
bright shirtings was from his blue-handed boys.
Each class became a family by its distinctness
not from the other, which it had as well,

but by the differences its people might have
known where they had lived. Each family was
pure in the way that anything is pure when it is
distant from another thing that might have touched it.
If your family had suffered purely, you were
nowhere, like the figures in a photograph that's been
retouched to rid it of the blurs they'd left
because they'd been too close or hadn't posed.
If there'd been just that single difference between
yourselves and the bourgeois, you wouldn't have been out
below the gaslamps on Blackfriars Bridge and seen
the plane of brickwork past Victoria that held
exactly to the river as it came toward you.
The tall mill-chimneys would have been so much the
unexampled symbols of your lot that you would
not have looked at them nor heard your clogs along
the gritstone paving as you crossed in front of
Renshaw's to the geese and elbowed past the men with
billy pots and mufflers, women in their shawls.
Clerks who were hopeful of a partnership were
not there with you if their difference from you
was that one simple difference. No one was
with you in that crowd if what it meant to
be there was one's solvency or lack of it,
those categorical reliefs from what was there
around you to be known. People were there and in the way.
If there hadn't been those differences that
place us where we are, you would have been no more
in Fennel Street or Rochdale Road among the stalls
than in a garden with the Gregs or Cunliffe-Listers.

Those who'd made their landed marriages were
interested in your condition. Everyone was
interested in your condition, some of them
afraid that you would have enough of it and turn it
back on them. They envied you your "profligate
remorseless and unteachable behavior." And they
lost how you were different among yourselves.
You concealed from one another what you didn't have
and color-stoned your doorsteps as your properties.
"Anyone who did not own a hat would fold himself
a low square paper cap," but you were cruel to
dwarfs and cripples as the Methodists were cruel to you.
You hated sheenies, socialists, and any who were
"getting on." You'd found your ways to classify
within that undermass the simplest differences,
and what that let you miss kept you alive.
Since it was dense and fractured, raw, too small,
your masters left you to the world you'd made for them.
Their way out of the ignorable was to find other
places in the empire — St. Lucia, Trinidad, Lahore.
England had outgrown the continent of Europe.
Free Trade was Jesus Christ. They formed their
joint-stock companies and combines and could count on
triple rows of sheds, eight miles of granite docks,
calm and deep water in all tides at Liverpool.
They were still in that plain geography of
"things in their places," of bales on
hoisting-pulleys and in ship-holds and, along the quays,
the dry white scudding that they lost as waste.
They were looking for those samenesses that make us feel we've

broken through to something, through those
unsure things that happen in a place in time to
something like our safe impalpable and self-sustaining
plans that are always future. With the rhythms of storage,
their great facades in Portland Street had alternating
arched or pedimented windows, glass-roofed wells where
buyers chose their cottons in an even light and then
went on to the Exchange by Parker Street and George
to Market through the uniform four-storied rows of
offices and shops that lined the thoroughfares and hid
the workers' quarters and the inland ports and passed below
The London & North-Western trunk lines out of
Ardwick Station south at easy gradients across
five bridges to the fields.

      Suppose we'd want to memorize the present.
We'd begin with a scenario and follow it
toward ourselves from some one point that's both
beyond us and contained within our past. By
this time, it would say, our stock of capital is
constant. The Secretariat does not coerce. Instead,
it monitors and guides toward their optimum
the populations and economies of all the disparate
subnational and local interests. Behind its
sure administration lies the aggregate of what we
know and go on learning. We'd known we needed
families for all the different things we learned,
and so we'd organized them on some trees, in two
dimensions, like the trees that show our lineage with

names for leaves, with room enough between the cousins
so that all of them might marry and be fruitful.
Somewhere, casually, we'd found a branch that was an
axis, a manifold of what we could imagine if we
changed the metaphor and made it deeper, used
more of what was there and empty, filled it
evenly with boxes, drawers, a drawer for every
class of possibility and Possibility
itself a drawer, and Cost, Location, Schedule,
Shape, Who Makes It, How It Moves — as many
drawers for any plan as there were matrices
within each drawer for each particular that held
discretely to itself within its matrix, then
aligned or didn't as we made our runs to find
the one least suspect way to bring it off.
This paradigm was Zwicky's. He applied it to his
telescopes to know what driving gears he'd need, what
vacuum pumps. To know within what fraction of a
wavelength of light his lenses should be polished.
Which cameras and spectrographs. Which of the
photoelectronic fields that pull each impulse
through to a magnet that resolves, refocuses and
sharpens it. The proper domes and mountings, screens.
Which engineers would build him the most stable
groundwork for the whole affair, with lateral
steel bracing as they use in dams. And where to
put it. Palomar. Mt. Wilson. Places where the
night sky glow from spectral lines and bands was
minimal, and where the winds in upper strata wouldn't
blur what he could see of supernovae bursting

37

outward toward quiescent faint blue stars. He
knew that's what they'd do. If he were thorough,
anything would do within its randomness what he could
plan that it would do. It helped if one knew how to
simulate a world, the way von Kármán did.
His tunnel was a closed system. It had its
own supply of air and kept returning it in one
uninterrupted flow across the surfaces of
streamlined wings and cowlings. In that thin
layer of air around them, he had found imaginary
drains and faucets that would change the flow and
shock their plane to spasms. He'd found the
Vortex Street, the drag on slender bodies like
the trout that Sir George Cayley watched in 1840 in a
pool below some shallows. Sand and fuller's earth had
shifted along the bottom, settled. With its
nose against the current, in its hold, the trout was a
spindle with diminishing resistance toward the tail.
Von Kármán often climbed inside his tunnel.
. He'd lie out flat. He'd feel the way the flow would
touch him if he were the trout, "a well-fed fish of
thirteen ounces" and a length that Cayley had
divided into thirds and measured for their mean
diameters. Von Kármán knew that these diameters were
basic. They were the girths at common points along the
profile of a new design. The Bell X-1 conformed almost
exactly. And the Flying Wing. Rockets were something
else again. He leased an office from a former
Vita-juice dispenser, Henry Gibbel. He took in
Zwicky as his partner. He called the corporation

Aerojet and worked on tracking, staging, and the two
propellants that had blasted through a Cal Tech wall.
He'd had to move his people when that happened —
Frank Malina, Hsue-shen Tsien, John Parsons, Amo Smith.
He'd set them up where JPL is now, in the low
dry hills behind the Devil's Gate impoundment and the
spillway to the channel draining south beyond
the Vista del Arroyo where the nurses walked with
burned skin-grafted veterans of World War II.
He'd helped to plan the arsenals of Germany, Japan and
China, Russia, the United States. He always came back
home to Pasadena, to his sister Pipö and the
house he'd bought when he'd been lured away from
Aachen in the twenties. His lab off San Pasqual looked
residential and benign among the dorms with
courtyards, cool arcades, the same pale stucco as the
whitewashed or adobe walls of mansions
south of California. In wedges of streets
west from the Huntington, the luxury of deeper lots was
trees, those full tall stands of them on slopes
behind the houses and the arbors with their loud
wisteria and peacocks, trees that from the streets were
backdrops for the pantiled roofs, for changing
attitudes and depths from house to house with one house
east a bit and closer to the curb, the next
less forward, taller, with a drying lawn, more shade,
the house itself no deeper on its lot than
his on South Marengo where he entertained
Niels Bohr, where Einstein stayed when he was here,
and Fermi. Pasadena was a semiarid

garden of trees. From the higher ground of Raymond Hill
east and north, from that corner of the city
out into the blocks of smaller lots across the five
flat miles from Eaton Wash to the Arroyo,
trees were the earned release from industry and from
the hot and bright long afternoons. Below
Millard and Poppyfields and Chaney Trail, there had been
orchards mostly with an interspersed few streets of
modest bungalows for the retired Mid-Western
patrons of the cafeterias downtown. By private
rights-of-way and by electric motive power,
they'd take the Red Car from the cemetery to the
sheds below St. Andrews, transfer to the stop at
Mission and Fair Oaks and change again and pass
the Ostrich Farm and follow the Arroyo
down toward the river and across it to the
terminal at Sixth and Main. Clifton's was a short walk.
Its waterfalls and grottos and lanais were less
peculiar to them now. They'd wait in line for trays,
then choose their dishes, pay, and share a table
always with another couple, the talk among them
friendly but uncomforting, designed to show
too much that they weren't lonely here and didn't miss
the state societies, their picnics in suburban parks,
signs on the trees to help them find themselves, and
buttons, Hog and Hominy, A Jayhawk, Flicker Tail,
the roll-calls of the counties and a speech,
then singing all together at the last about a
"land with its sweet-scented plains." It didn't
matter that they loved the new, they sang, they'd

"not forget the old." The trains had brought so
many of them out to "do" the state that they'd been sold
themselves and one another. There were the tours to
studios and missions and the beaches and to
Alpine Tavern on the Mt. Lowe run. They'd seen
everything and more, and what it came to for them was
the building that was going on, a growth they could
explain by all those landmarks and the days. They'd bought
into it and moved and stayed and found they'd left more
changes than they'd known they had. Their sense of
where they lived depended strangely on their
fitness to change, as if they couldn't know
without those changes where they were or what they
wanted in their lives. Living here was too much what they'd
thought it would be. The sequences of perfect days were
unavoidably what they'd come for. They should be making
more of what was there and possible at any
hour in that clear air. With all those possibilities
aligned for them along the tracks and poles and wires,
they should be somewhere else since where they were was
old already with their being there. There was an oldness
too about the Echo Mountain Incline to Professor Lowe's
observatory, about his searchlight that was visible
100 miles at sea, about his zoo and the museum.
His line went on toward the crest on trusses,
concrete piers. He'd planned to build across a gorge
a swinging cable railway to a great hotel,
but when his notes came due he couldn't pay.
The route from Rubio to Crystal Springs became
another of the trips that Huntington could sell on his

"Day for a Dollar" trolleys, 6,000 daily runs
from Redlands through the citrus groves to San
Fernando, out to Venice and to Orange over enough
wide-gauge track between the stops to reach
Nebraska or Hidalgo del Parral. The rails were
older than the growth that was the only solvent
business in the place. If those dispersed connected
cities didn't grow, there wasn't anything but
piped-in water, rails, electric power. It had to
grow by filling in. It couldn't do that on the old
fixed lines alone but needed rents and markets,
interests, more ways to make the land less simply
there and waiting to be bought. When it was bought
again, for more, at little down, good terms,
it brought its benefits to everyone from
that large trust that this was where to live.
The plans for roads could speak of trains with some
nostalgia. They had done so much. There would be fewer
grade crossings, fewer delays for trains because fewer trains,
more Chevrolets and Fords. Cars would take people
anywhere. At their own times and by themselves,
at greater intervals according to their speeds,
more people drove each day across the new
divisions of the ranchos on the secondary
highways, local streets, the points each car would pass
no newer for that difference. The empty lots were
old with impossibility. They were sometimes
salted with a pile of sand or bricks to look more
promising to buyers. The land itself didn't
go anywhere. Places were old. The things that

filled them had been planned and paid for, the profits
counted already, reinvested, spent, passed by.
Bungalows were less in fashion than the spanishy
flat shuttered fronts, wrought-iron bars and spears
and balconies with canvas awnings, doors with the ornate
churrigueresques that public buildings had and
movie houses, filling stations, churches, and the stores.
This was their Colonial Revival. It was
old in what it missed, that native aristocracy of
landed dons. Its counterpart ten years before had been the
Greene & Greenes whose oil- and soap-rich clients wanted
liberal free-standing houses that disclaimed the
sources of their wealth. The Greenes, like Morris, wanted
well-made things for everyone and wanted everyone to
make them, if they could. Cal Tech was still
Throop Polytechnic. It taught both sexes
carpentry and turning, architectural design.
The students learned to sew and weave and worked with
leather, clay, and metals. George Ellery Hale would
change that. From the Greenes' own patrons he had won
endowments for his telescope and for the funds it took
to bring more science to the school. He could foresee
pure research and technology as complementary
twin halves. The region was cut off. It needed
fuel and water, power. Geologists and engineers would
pay for one another's futures, for the futures too of
climatology and astrophysics. The future was
successive and successful answers to those
questions it made sense to ask. How far from the
earth itself could we project? And what was light?

In the calculus of variations, what was the mean
process of behavior in a species, in a
social class? Could we compute a place for
each of us within the equalizing
sameness of plan? If we overlooked nothing,
no single difference of temperament or will,
if it were all accounted for and stored and if we
watched it periodically and found it yielded
more and newer orders, it would teach us how to
master what was probable and make it pure,
assign it a completeness like the past's. It would be
pain alone that held its place, that couldn't be
planned away from that one body that was living it in
hope, not waiting, not afraid to know it wasn't
worth it, all that pain. It was worth it. There were
people who made it worth it, and the world. A cat came
sleepily from a thick shrub and stopped and shook its head.
There was time between the bleatings of the horn to be
reminded and forget again the huckster and his fish
two streets away, then one, then out of hearing, gone,
the shadows of the fences less alert as the heat gave
way a little and the peas were shucked, all changes
watched for now as if one were confined and sitting up
in bed, alone, with nothing but the afternoon
outside along the ground toward the lilac and the
cactus in the foothills. The room didn't have that
loneliness of rooms she'd stopped to notice in her
haste to get her gloves or hat, rooms where she'd
asked herself how lonely it would be to have to
stay there for the afternoon and not go out.

She was reading about North Borneo, about a
concentration camp, the Japanese, their curious
honor and the cruelty that came from it. She hadn't
seen that in them, doubted it. She wondered what the
spareness of the things they'd lived with meant to
sailors on the carriers. The glare outside was
just what they would have stared through for their Zeros.
From the promenade, on each crossing, late,
later than this, she'd watched the clouds curve up in
tumbles that had brought no wind. Alone, it had been like
seeing a place for someone else whom one might never
tell about it, filled, as one was, with the colored
presence of what was there, with how it all spread
back and away and rounded, shone, went dim.
It filled one with the ease of trusting that the
other person too was in a place. Nor was it lonely
here. Her chair. The dressing table. Desk.
A blue slip cast ware and a single tile.
Light from beyond the hedges through the mica
panels in the shade, the lamp arresting it,
steadying for that last rush of sun that left her wanting
nothing more, not the lamp itself for reading nor the
food her mother brought, fresh vegetables and custard.
Elva. She was Elva. Under the one twilight,
the Esterbrooks' on Allen, Helen Thayer's, the tiny
cottage of the Kelsos' in the trees behind the
Elk's Club. Las Lunas, the McGowans'. Peg and Herb
Cheeseborough. The Hezleps. Orville. Allie Lou.
There were others who were more like family — Lucile,
Florence and Glen. Jimmie was at Lucile's.

Jim would be driving home from downtown past
Elysian Park and through the tunnels, past the glazed
deep pocket of the reservoir he might not see.
It was dim already in her bungalow at school,
the pasteboards in their slots, the sheets of rough
construction paper sorted by their shades and sizes.
Both rooms smelled like sweeping-compound, glues,
like the stark poster-paints in jars with white lids.
Occasionally, a car would turn from Madre onto Del Mar,
behind it and ahead along the streets
the separate conversations in the houses, trysts,
an evening with the radio. The sky was a pale wash.
It caught outside the windows all the late
small matters on the lawns, and lights inside were coming on
too soon.

    No sleep for either of us on the flight to
Maine and then to Gatwick. From the train, back yard
allotments and cooperatives, the city hardly
there at all outside Victoria and there inside it
only as a crowd. It's hot, of course, and everyone
just manages. We pass them in their queues. They need
maps and bookings, taxis, other trains. I try to think they
like some part of this. It would help me through the raw
worry of what to do if I could think they
liked it in some way I didn't. I ask about the
Grosvenor, and it's silly to have asked because it's
here, inside the station. We take our bags upstairs,
come down again, go out to look for dinner, eat,

come back and go to sleep. When I hear it, I know
first that it's coming from below, from that odd warm
hollow where the people were and where they must be now,
still purposeful and hearing differently this voice.
A woman's, young, it names in series all the single
destinations, platforms, times, then carries here with
nothing that disturbs me, nothing I can understand,
no word, with nothing lost, no listening and only
letting go, forgetting.

It's rarely that easy. The ease of it has
little to do with how tired I am. If it's before
midnight, if there's still time enough to sleep,
I go to sleep. At two or three, when I wake up,
I have to be asleep again within an hour.
I shouldn't let it bother me. Even if I
don't go back to sleep, I shouldn't worry that I haven't
slept enough, that I'll feel it in my eyes. If my
tongue won't work, if it makes me slur the things I
press myself to say, I'll say just that much less.
I should ignore all day in what I do each
thought of myself and how I'm feeling tired.
I work at my breathing for a while, listen to
Linda's and adopt it, a sleeper's breathing.
Mine would be slower. To breathe the way she breathes,
I'd have to be awake, and am, have been awake
too long now and have given up on trying to know
exactly what I should be doing, how I could be
thinking about it all and changing. So I don't

care if I go back to sleep. Since it never works to
care about it, since my calmness when I care is
feigned and crazy, I don't care. I'll get up.
I'm too tired to get up, I'll give up here. And even the
giving up is trying, a counterfeit that takes me into
harmless things, a seagull, my socks, into the drowse of
someone giving up who meets that first improbable
ellipsis, slips beyond it to a second and a third and,
losing count, goes off between the scatter, sleeps,
is someone who's asleep, not me at all, who's only
almost there and pleased to be this close, too pleased,
now coming to my hold again with all the shifts
intact and unrelieved. I've lost my chance.
Having been so close and missed, I can't start over.
Nor can I trust that even now I've given up.
I'm left remembering the times I've gone to sleep,
and what I've done each time is to forget.
It's happened before. I've slept. I was asleep an
hour ago when nothing woke me, when I was simply
awake. I didn't have to see that it was still
too dark. To know I wasn't where I'd been
two nights ago, or one, Les Bouilladoires, Cassis,
I didn't have to hear inside my head the
syllables of Juan-les-pins. It might be different if
once for any fraction of that irreversible one
moment I could be unsure. If I had to sort through
where I was and was it time, if there were
sequence or change, some need to tell myself I'd
done it again — that for another night, and here,
again, impossibly, I'd placed myself too soon —

then I'd have doubted, sleep would have given me
doubt, resisted me a little, made me wait,
kept me for just that long from knowing that it's
me who brings this on and can't undo it, who won't
live it as it is, as mine. The certainty that
sleep isn't there is me. At angles, in
parentheses and stacks, my waking pulls me on
from this to that and this and I can't
stop them or go back or choose, they're all the
same to me, I make them all the same by
hating them for keeping me awake. Each part is my
excuse to be sure. It lets me prove that there are
others like itself, that I can be replacing it with
others, each itself replacing what I want until I'm
sure that I won't have it, sure that wanting sleep is
helplessly safe. Since sleep is all I want, there's
nothing else that I'm removed from. Wanting is a bore.
I can distract myself, contrive a lustful graphic
time of it and feel it take, my penis, by degrees,
my proof that things can change. It's more like
doing something to get up and walk. The bathroom door,
the light. Although I've taken it too many times, my
doing this can be a start. I spill them in my palm.
Fourteen. They're grainy and pale, a uniform
clear score across each face. This one. When it works,
it's like a tiredness I take inside me. It
weakens and breaks, dissolves inside me in a
gradual prolonged slow carry into sleep.
It isn't tiredness. I'd have it to go
back to if it were. I'd trust it as a need.

I'd do what willing sleep won't let me do,
I'd rest between my tiredness and sleep and
wait for them to take me. I'd feel them
measure, as I came away, my heading toward.
Repeatably, on either side of sleep, there'd be a
time that I could wait for. Going either way, I'd
wait and be pleased. It would be time to be
awake now, time to sleep, my tired surmises
tired of themselves and me and, given up,
forgotten in my rest. It's my remembering that
tires me when I'm doing badly, doing what I'd
willed I wouldn't do again — the same embarrassing
explosion over nothing much, self-pity, fear.
I've willed too often that I wouldn't be afraid,
that I would quit my way of thinking
backward from a safer time, the symptom or the threat
behind me then, the drive and its risk survived.
My going somewhere wouldn't be my getting
past it in time, past it to my staid, more certain
memory of how it was, of how my wanting
not to be afraid had tired me, made it hard to
start at any time with what was left. I miss the
steadiness I sometimes have that lets me
stop and go back, begin to choose, defer to
patience and surprise and incompleteness, loss, to
versions of things, the sense we follow when we're
talking to a friend and knowing that he
understands us, wants to tell us too a
story that he wouldn't tell if we'd been
with him all the time. There isn't time for stories,

there's too much. My friends aren't here, and I'm
forgetting what I meant to ask or tell them
yesterday, the day before. And when it
matters that I try to keep it, when I
prop it with its mattering and call it up
again, another time, I feel it isn't
theirs anymore, it's mine, and it's too dear, I
keep it with the others that I've blurred and kept,
the dead ridiculous and grand collection all I
know about my time. I write to someone,
you. I say I like it here. I say that I'm confused.
I know these rifts and these delays are still
forgivably ahead, that I can start.
The differences we don't catch up with aren't the
incubus I make them be by wanting
always, all the time, a hold I don't
forgive myself for wanting. So I want something else.
I want my balance to be alternately
there and not, the way it is when I'm up
walking somewhere and forget my weight —
around me, and in balance, in the world,
the things I'll never think about or see.

　　He says he's Antony, no "h," they've spelled it
wrong on the card he shows me, someone in this
hospital has spelled it wrong. It's Thursday. He says
tomorrow they will tell him when it's time.
He'll start to fold his clothes and put them in his
suitcase — first the pants he isn't wearing, then

his underpants and socks. He'll wear a different shirt. So
this one that he's wearing now, he'll fold it too —
this sleeve across, this other one. He'll put it in his
suitcase, on the top, his shirts are last. He'll pull the
zippers all the way until it's closed and then he'll
lift it by its handles, carry it across the rug. The
door will be there, he'll open it. He'll go on through the
hallway to the door and open it and come inside toward that
other door. He'll go on through it to the
anteroom, the door and steps, the car. He'll put his
suitcase on the seat behind his mother, close the door.
He'll get inside the car, in front, he'll close the door.
I want to let him tell me all of it. I want to
wait to hear the things he'll do and let it
please me that he'll do them. And he will. He will be
back here, after Sunday, every week, and every
Friday he'll go home. But I'm not listening, I'm
ahead of him or still behind, he's in his
bedroom with his clothes unpacked and then he's
folding them to come back here, he's Antony, his
name-card again, it's Thursday, then his clothes, and I
excuse myself. He says good-by as if he knows he's
told me enough, I could have stayed but he's not
sorry that I'm going. Or I've made that up. Because it
sticks for him and won't go on without his
thinking what he'll do, I want him to be
used to something. Even if it's being left, if
that's what he's used to, or the place. Another
visitor who listens and then leaves is
habit for him, he's been left again, he has to

start with that each time or give up being
used to being heard. A lady's saying
hello to him now, he's telling her his name.
Rehearsing what he wants to feel he's up to
helps him, makes it all right. It's all right,
it's not too much for him, these Fridays. Almost
beyond him, in the car, his mother asks him is he tired,
would he like a nice cream gateau after lunch.
She knows it's hard for him to listen. He can't be
ready enough to hear what someone says, it can't
belong to him, it shifts, keeps coming in and
tires him with its wanting to be heard.
Beyond him, almost easily, the traffic and the stops,
the roundabouts for Market Drayton, rain, the M.
Her trouble at the exit is too far away,
too close, he can't align it, doesn't try, it isn't
here, inside him, like his knowing he should wait,
she hasn't told him yet. They're still not there,
and now they are, she's told him, he should start.
He's on his feet outside the car. The door doesn't
catch at first, and then it does, and each
disturbance through the last unfolded pants is
very near, it's next, it's here, he meets it as the
wave of deeper places that he can't make fit.
She's switched his dresser and his bed and it's all right.
Behind this change, the little more that he might
look at, sometime, from his room. His curtains lean
abruptly onto nothing — light, the day, the different points,
whatever he excludes that otherwise would
stop him forever as its dumb too thorough

index of how much there is. If it's fine, he'll go out
into it on Sunday. His father doesn't
mention any more that they're out walking through the
Brynlow wood. They see the butcher and they
keep right on, hello, and yes it's lovely, yes he did,
did he? At the escarpment, when they wait,
he doesn't know his father sees some farms,
the Pennines to the right, and Stockport, Hyde, the Greater
Manchester conurbation, its line below the moors
less generalized than how it looks on mid-scale
insets in the Irish Sea. The world is plural
only as it shows what each of us sees differently.
Inside its different aspects it's the same.
We try to get inside what lies between
the ways it looks to us and how it is.
We want to know it. Maps are a way
of bringing into sympathy and our control
all levelings and projections on its curved replete
outside. We sink the benchmarks, measure
sides to another benchmark. We take our
stereoscopic pairs of pictures from the air and
scan them for a true relief. When we've composed
one scale from which the others all derive,
we print in stages with the different plates
these lines and colors, these details. The map for drivers
simplifies the contour. It supposes that
obliquely, from the northwest corner,
sunlight in its wedge is giving us a bleached
readable surface. The single sheet has
Scotland on the other side. In three languages,

the legend to the left explains that there are
primary destinations. These have been marked.
Between them, with their distances, an interlaced
blue for the motorways with green and red.
The numbers of the routes don't interrupt the
junctions or the names of towns. Slopes that face
away from the light are shaded in a freehand grey that's
heaviest along a ridge. There are spot-heights. We can
see that the Norfolk Broads are flat, and the fens,
that the clays and chalks all differ from the
uplands somehow. To hint at any more than that would
darken it. Places we'd be driving would recede,
their script too timid. The series of seventeen
Quarter-inch sheets is solid color — light green and
yellows for the lower ground, then buffs. Among
other codes in the margin, a totem helps us know how
high we are if we're on crosshatched beige.
It's a busier map. The rails are black, there's black
stippling for the cities. Its overlay of roads is
blue again, and red, and brown. It shows us the lanes,
the narrow tracks with passing places. Steep grades are
arrows with their tips downhill. We'd use a much
larger scale to walk by, larger than the old red-covered
Inch-to-a-mile, and brighter, with no hill-shading, only
outlines of relief on a blank ground, and fewer
meddlesome details. We'd carry the sheet
with us as a prod to keep us looking for the
footpaths that it says are there. If we'd left the car
just off the A-road and had done all right,
if the trace along a wall had led us clearly to

another in another field, and so on, and it was
fresh there, damp at our feet and drying in the wind,
we might be starting to forget it wasn't ours.
The gates that ask us please to close them, latches that work,
a huge horse-chestnut in the line of hedge across to
that slight rise, the barn there, rooks, "all the fine
cattle going about that would do your heart
good to see" — it isn't ours or any Cheshire
dairy-farmer's. It's the map's, a pure informed
plotting of the rights-of-way through features we can
bear on when it all goes wrong. Where the path's been
lost to a tractor that had ploughed close up, or where
the hay's been cut, where we're left with only stubble,
when we see, beyond the windows, at the copse,
a stile or a gate and cross toward it and it's
neither, just the fence, and more of it, around us, here,
there's still the way we came. From the disused
railway that we passed, or from the hill, we'll line up
Bexton and the Toft Hall spire. We've overlooked a whole
miscellany of clues. It makes us want the next
larger scale again, and the next, their narrowing
systems of intelligence on how the ground arranges
outcrop and cliffs, loose boulders, intergraded
trees over coppice over scrub. The river's been
moved a little to the right so we can read the
mean high water and the low, the pumping stations,
weirs and sluices. Roads at this scale are still assigned
conventional widths. Only when we've started
in from the country, when the path in the grass verge is
sidewalk and it's mapped, when the treads of the

steps are mapped, and the curbs, and we can follow
house by house the numbers or the names, Japonica,
Pendennis, Lucknow, Manor Dene — only at twenty-five
inches to the mile are the strips that take us places
truer to plan. We measure ourselves, we know how
broad we are at the hips or shoulders and we're
there on the map, provisionally, in scale.
We see exactly what allowances we'd have to
either side if we were centered, if there were few enough
people on the streets that we could center ourselves
exactly. It's what we try to do outside the
Royal Exchange, or on the ramp to an upper
story of a car-park. In adjacent sheets, the map
shows us these things to scale. Each permanent
feature on the ground is shown to scale until, at
1:1250, it's easier to list what isn't there:
tombstones and vaults; small sheds in private gardens;
signal-posts in the neighborhood of a large
marshaling yard, like Ardwick; repetitive things —
letter boxes, transmission lines on single poles,
bollards and capstans on the Salford quay.
We're shown in plan the thickness of an outer wall,
its juts and its recesses, where it thins.
If they're five square meters or more, we see, from the top,
all courtyards, light or ventilation shafts,
each well in the Portland St. storerooms crossed with the
symbol for a glass-house roof. We don't really see
inside. Even at this largest scale, we're shown
nothing in the way of rooms. We know from the
Bureau of the Censuses that rooms are surely

countable and counted, that people are themselves
accounted for, by survey, with their clear consent,
in confidence. All subjects are assured that they've been
chosen at random, they're a sampling, maybe it's
where they live, or their job, the interviewer isn't
sure, really. May she come inside? She needs their
age and sex, are they married, what type of a
household is it, how many people here are
catered for at least five nights each week by the
same person? Are they employed? At what? Would they
look at this chart and say within which group their net
income is likely to fall? How much and what kind of
education have they had? Is this a detached or
semidetached or terraced house, a flat? And how many
rooms are there? There might be questions too about
amenities and cars and contraceptives, episodes of
physical and mental illness, deaths. They're asked for their
opinions, sometimes, and are probed. Could they explain more
fully? In what way? Some answers are foreseen and we
precode them. Or we close the terms. "Here are
six sorts of behavior. Which would you disapprove of
most in a married man, a friend of yours, who is
not in the police?" We frame the things they say. When they're
compatibly and cleanly numbered, we can run them through.
To any number we can always add one
because it works that way, by adding numbers.
Because it's small, because our maps for it are much
larger than its surface, we've learned to print in
silicon, on chips, an integrated plane of
microchannels, spurs and gates. Its circuitry will run

twelve thousand operations in an inch,
the bits, with their addresses, there, inside,
not going very far. Because it remembers
perfectly, because it never sleeps, because it can
sort and compare and choose and find the proper
order in the sum of all its pulses, ON or OFF,
the things they say in eighteen million homes are
digitized and stored, revised, called up again by
GEOCODE with its coordinates for any point
P on the map, all references on grid and bearing
east and north in equal squares from their false origin.
We're somewhere in its mesh of cells and always
catching up. There's always, just ahead of us, a
rate or table, an estimate of trends that we
belong to and that waits. We watch it as we watch ourselves,
expectantly, afraid that in the calculus of
pain and pleasure, at the scale of 1:1, we're not
happy enough. To be happy, we have to be sure.
We'd be surer if enough of us were happy.
This many will kill themselves, this many won't,
or we'll be off a little in our reckoning.
As predicates of what's been well-rehearsed,
we're either well- or ill-behaved. To help us know
the different points of stress at different times, we're
averaged out, depicted from the top with all our
furnishings — and there are scripts. The stir at breakfast.
Sandwiches are being cut. We see how much room
Mother needs at the work-top when someone else
passes behind her with a tray. The toddler wanders
in and out of the kitchen as she tidies up. She's

bathing him now, lifting him from the tub: is the floor
wide enough here for her to towel him dry?
We need our clearances and kinds of peace from
sideboards and chairs, settees, rectangular or round
coffee tables. They steady us, these things we've made.
We move between them, retrieve a sameness from the same
bookcase, the same clock. People don't always want to
watch TV when it's on. They need a place to sit
away from it so they can talk or read. And in the
bedroom? Should they try it with more pillows?
Standing up? What is it that might singularly
please them there as they imagine it being
better than the last time, than the best?
Is it how she'd seem to know before he asked,
or that her breathing as she came would take him too?
In the quantum of their parts and how they move,
where are they when they've started? His cock's
inside her and they've started, her labia
just visible around him on the outward strokes.
It troubles us that we don't quite see to the
heart of a place. Whatever shows itself
conceals its other sides and how it works.
She's leaning on her hands, astride him, her face
strained and turned away as, in and out, more
surely now, he feels her start to ease beyond this
time they're keeping. He tries to slow her but she's
past it, past her wanting. And as she comes,
it's like the wakefulness she leaves when he's been
holding her and waiting and her shudder tells him
now, now she's asleep, she's left him, and he comes.

Equal, complete, their bodies are as far away as
outer is from inner, then from now. As if for
each of them inside their separate minds
there was another who was listening to them think,
they're not so much alone as by themselves.
They're thinking. Neither speaks. Infinity being a
funny number, we lose them to themselves as each
remembers and awaits, concurrently, from
anywhere in time and nowhere yet, another
part of what they're thinking or a pause.

      We've rented this house for seven years.
I keep thinking of the back yard as something I could
know but don't have time to, it would take too long, I'm too
busy at school, or here, or we're away, I
postpone it, save it for a time when I'll have more
peace with my nerves. When I'm doing the dishes,
I look out at it and remember some of the names,
eugenia at the kitchen window, flagstones,
St. Augustine. There's a jasmine border with three
squat confused palm-trees, oleander, a sundial,
a cement squirrel. Since it's something I can
do there, I like to mow the tiny matted lawn.
The bathroom the Brainerds added on in 1964
pinches and shades the clothesline. We cut the holly
back from it, and the pittosporum too. And on the
longer days, in May, before we leave, the sheets are
dry in an hour. If I were simply to
watch them for that time, if I watched a bottom

corner of one sheet and waited while it kept
bending and going slack, I'd be hearing
Coast Highway, tires in a lane, a truck, more cars,
too many for me to tell which way any
one of them was coming. I can sometimes tell at night.
If I've heard it for a while before it's here,
it's from the left. Place Realty mutes it.
So do the trees in the ravine. Coming from the
other side, it's past Cabrero's fence before I
hear it at all. I listen to it go away.
Another from the right, a few more. And then none.
A gap between them always sounds much longer than it
ought to be. It makes me strain to hear
through it to the next car. Or maybe I'm thinking
backward to the last ones, wanting to hear them
south now in front of the trailer park, and north, in town.
It's late enough that the roads seem less like the
same one road. A certain interchange — like each
wide flat bridge across the next dry river, it's
almost a place. Or the Canyon. Driving it now with their
brights on, they watch the shrubs for lights of
cars coming the other way. They feel their dimmers
click when they press them, click as their brights come
on again when they've passed. The drivers didn't
see anything of one another's faces.
What do we see of people from our cars?
Ahead of me on a road through small farms,
two couples who've stopped to talk. They walk to the side.
Looking back at them in the mirror, I can tell I've
broken up their meeting. It's early and very cold,

and I can see the words between them as they leave.
Where a tractor had turned out onto the road,
an arc of dried mud. My tires throw it
up against the undercarriage and there's
snow in the furrows between the new shoots,
on the corrugated roof of a shed, its gutters
dripping a little. I was seeing what was easier.
A farmhouse, pollarded trees, the rest of it,
it was easier than seeing people. At the far edge,
beyond the fields, the tall flared top of another
water-castle. People were going on
forgettably with what they did, but not right there.
The postman was there in his yellow truck. He had his
route to do, I knew that much about him.
Housewives were in the shops on their various
errands and charges and were coming back
out into the cold. An hour or so before,
I'd seen them in the square, in Mirepoix. They were
all I'd had to go on. Waiting in the car, I'd watched
this one or that as she shifted what she carried,
took the step to the arcade and disappeared.
I'd noticed a Citroën, how its steering
kneels to the side it's turned to when it's parked.
Then Linda, with our lunch, and we'd been on our
way again by the map on another day of seeing
just what we wanted to, whatever we could,
vineyards still, and farms, a walled city, I was letting
signs and the names of places as they came
withdraw to the place which then itself withdrew,
the next one to the next as seamlessly as if

none of it were missing. Except when I was
with them on the streets, it wasn't like people, like those
junctures with them when I think they might be
looking at me too. To someone who lived there,
what was I doing in Morbegno? How long would I stay?
Coming back through town each day to our one room.
Winter, a mountain to the south, noon. The sun was
glory for that hour we had it and I walked on
into it, its channel between the fronts
three stories deep. In the glare from bricks laid
vertically in swirls on the steep street, people were the
sounds they made. A woman. We passed. Even in her haste
she may have seen my strangeness. I couldn't tell.
It would have been all right for her to look,
I couldn't have seen her looking. It's usually
not all right. We shouldn't stare. In cities
our mix is random. We glut the streets with intricate
crossed-glances at things, a news-rack, a display.
If we belong there, we don't want people to
see that we see their faces. Sometimes they do.
Is something wrong? they seem to ask us when we're caught.
We cover it up. For as long as we can, we hide.
And what do they want who look at us? They want what
we want — sex, or talk, whatever's missing,
whatever we look to fill. We can't always know.
What the derelict want is usually too clear.
They halloo us with their eyes and we're ashamed,
we pay them so they won't keep looking. They
eat the shame and drink it, they survive, they stay
shameful for us, they show us that our needs are

shameful, that we agree to that, that even they agree.
We see them crying to themselves on benches in the sun.
They walk the gutters. Alone and talking loudly,
screening their mouths with their hands so we won't hear,
they step to the sidewalk, accost someone
ahead of us on the sidewalk, whom we pass, listening,
wanting to hear what they say. We should give up our
places, they say, they've given up theirs.
The person they've stopped tries to keep his place.
I tried to keep mine with a lady in Fulham Road.
She was saying "Can you help me, are you
important enough to help me? You look important,
will you marry me?" She said we'd share. She was a
seer now, she saw through stories to the All-at-once.
Where I was born, and when, how I look, who my
friends are, what it falls to me to do — she could see
through all that to a deeper luck that was
hers and mine together while I heard. She wanted her
place back, could I help her, it was my luck too.
I wanted to show her that it wasn't. If she didn't
disgust me, there'd be little that we shared, I'd be
protecting her, she wouldn't have to see how helplessly
timid I was and self-estranged. I couldn't talk.
I was afraid to be disgusted. She could see.
Our hearts were there. Neither of us could hide.
And we were married by the awe that lay between.
I got away from her. I walked. The different streets
joined and went on obliquely and I followed them,
I didn't try to read them for their hearts.
Where should I go? Inside my template for the

stations and the parks and squares, I was getting my
place back. I'd gotten away from her, had to, even with
Linda sometimes I have to turn away from looks that go
on like that commandingly. With friends too. How long should I
hold your look or you mine? It's a time that's too certain,
that leaves too little room for the tacit
losses and trusts that are the time we live
away from our friends. Alone, we have to stay
used to ourselves so they'll know us. Have they changed?
We think what they're likely to be doing now,
with whom, and where. We think about their hearts.
Are we too important to them? Not enough?
Would they assure us that they're glad we're who we are?
I travel very badly after a while. Morning
and midday and evening and meals and
finding meals, finding a place to stay —
those are the junctures. I feel I'm what I
might have seen but didn't. Or what I might have found to
say about it all if there'd been time.
My longing for it now encloses it in my not
being there to let it get away. From here,
from this house we won't come back to after June,
I take my time remembering a walk.
Corners, a city block, the names, the typical
street-furniture and traffic. I could have
stopped outside the windows of the shops,
prolonged it, stayed alert, kept trying to absorb its
ordinary hidden business. Like the rest of them,
I'd gone on. We were all of us in the
middle of something. At her leisure,

looking at clothes, a girl with a bag, her other hand
behind her at the waist and holding lightly her
right elbow. People waiting to cross. With their first steps,
they were that much closer to my losing them.
To a question that I tried to overhear,
a woman answered at my back that, no, she didn't
think of herself as being bored. And the man who stretched
forward at the curb to see around me. Was he late?
What he was called to was another day,
to that one part of it I might have learned by asking.
Along the boulevards, in 1840, the flâneur
chatted with whom he pleased as casually as the
pace his turtle set him. I try to imagine him
subtler than that. Although he'd talk with them sometimes,
they'd rarely place him by the way he dressed
or by his preference for districts. Letting the crowd
inscribe him with its hurry and its looks,
he'd be its marker, watching — it would be by
him that we might figure who we are.
Disdainful, and preoccupied, and tired,
it's what we miss that makes us passers-by.
I meet someone. We talk. We're both a little
surprised that it's that easy. Am I sounding
too cordial, too relieved? It isn't
traveling that makes me ask, I do the same thing here.
I think too much beyond my part in what I'm saying.
Is this other person interested? I can't be sure.
To shame me out of wanting to be sure,
you've told me that you think I'd feel more
interesting if I were dying. That just might

do it, you think. It might remind me more that
I'm interested, me. I wouldn't lean so far
ahead of myself, I wouldn't have to,
I'd have my closure with me as I talked.
Maybe it's what I want. I hope you're wrong.
I still might ask you "Have I told you this before?"
We tell each other things that are only
starting to make sense. If they seem to make
more as we tell them, and if we go on,
what is it that we're leaving out? We're past it now.
Whatever it was, we didn't have to say it, didn't
break with it in the way that talking breaks
open, within it, between its parts, a time for
other parts, intrusions, more chances to be
missing what we meant to say. Linda was
awake one night and wanted to tell me where she'd
gone with them that afternoon. They'd parked at a
power station, where it was flat. There were tracks
already for their skis and they skied there until
Giorgio or Pironda thought they should go around
behind the village by some poplars and try it up
that way. The buildings thinned out and there were
sheds with animals with piles of straw outside and
men in some of the sheds and outside too with more
straw for the animals and bringing out the dung.
She had to go around bushes and small trees. She kept
falling, and they all laughed and decided to come
back through the village because it might be easier.
The street was ice and hardly wide enough for
two of them at a time, or for a cart.

They felt showy in their bright nylon.
A woman with a bowl looked at them from her door.
Chickens. A covered water-trough. She told me
more about the street and then remembered.
What she was saying, she said, was that there were
farmers out working in the snow.